Air Fryer, Coffee, Go

Delicious, Guilt-Free Air Fryer Breakfast
Recipes To Have A Good Morning

By
Lisa Gill

the publisher or the original author of this work can be in any fashion deemed liable for any hardship or damages that may befall them after undertaking information described herein.

Additionally, the information in the following pages is intended only for informational purposes and should thus be thought of as universal. As befitting its nature, it is presented without assurance regarding its prolonged validity or interim quality. Trademarks that are mentioned are done without written consent and can in no way be considered an endorsement from the trademark holder.

Table of Contents

Introduction

I think that much of my childhood memories are built around fried foods. The smell of crispy, battered fish and chips, homemade mozzarella sticks, burgers, shrimp, and so many other delicious fried foods tinge the memory of my mother and grandmother's houses. Many of the recipes that have been passed down through the generations in our family include at least one fried item but this was normal back then.

We didn't yet know how bad excessive amounts of oils, especially saturated fats, are for us. Today we have a huge amount of research and the historical data that is showing us that there is a reason that cardiovascular disease is the biggest cause of death globally—deficient diet. This doesn't just include fried foods, of course, but also all processed and junk foods, but if we cut out processed and junk food and still use a huge amount of bad fats in our cooking process, we aren't helping matters.

As a dietician, this knowledge was imparted on me during my studies, and I realized just how risky my generational family diet had been. It was at this moment I decided to change the way my own family ate. I was determined to send my children out into the world with a different idea about cooking than I had been taught.

At first, this meant that we had to cut out many of the foods we enjoyed because there simply wasn't a way to make them without cooking them in some form of fat. Soon, I discovered a kitchen appliance that changed my life — the air fryer. The most amazing thing about this appliance is that it doesn't just replace conventional frying, it also works for food that you would normally cook in an oven and in a fraction of the time!

The air fryer is a compact convection oven that fits on your countertop. It uses superheated air to cook foods that produce results very similar to deep-frying or roasting under high temperatures.
Depending on which brand you buy, the control set-up of your air fryer may differ slightly, but generally, the air fryer has three sets of controls that we need to look at.

- The temperature control dial
- The control panel
- The automatic timer button

The temperature control dial allows you to set the temperature your food will be cooked at. This range is most commonly anywhere between 175°F and 400°F. You can also adjust the cooking temperature during the cooking process.

One of the biggest concerns for air fryer beginners is that they won't know what temperature to use and how long to cook. Our recipes and this guide provide you with much of the required information and, it won't be long until you are confidently programming the air fryer yourself.

So what are you waiting for! Have fun cooking these fantastic and delicious air fryer recipes that are easy to prepare but full of flavor. Don't give up on a healthy lifestyle!

Egg and Bacon Muffins

Prep time: 5 minutes
Cook time: 15 minutes
Serves: 1

Ingredients:
- 2 eggs
- Salt and ground black pepper, to taste
- 1 tablespoon green pesto
- 3 ounces (85 g) shredded Cheddar cheese
- 5 ounces (142 g) cooked bacon
- 1 scallion, chopped

Directions:
1. Preheat the air fryer to 350°F (177°C). Line a cupcake tin with parchment paper.
2. Beat the eggs with pepper, salt, and pesto in a bowl.
3. Mix in the cheese.
4. Pour the eggs into the cupcake tin and top with the bacon and scallion.
5. Bake in the preheated air fryer for 15 minutes, or until the egg is set.
6. Serve immediately.

Breakfast Sausage and Cauliflower

Prep time: 5 minutes

Cook time: 45 minutes

Serves: 4

Ingredients:
- 1 pound (454 g) sausage, cooked and crumbled
- 2 cups heavy whipping cream
- 1 head cauliflower, chopped
- 1 cup grated Cheddar cheese, plus more for topping
- 8 eggs, beaten
- Salt and ground black pepper, to taste

Directions:
1. Preheat the air fryer to 350°F (177°C).
2. In a large bowl, mix the sausage, heavy whipping cream, chopped cauliflower, cheese and eggs.
3. Sprinkle it with salt and ground black pepper.
4. Pour the mixture into a greased casserole dish.
5. Bake in the preheated air fryer for 45 minutes or until firm.
6. Top with more Cheddar cheese and serve.

Parmesan Sausage Egg Muffins

Prep time: 5 minutes

Cook time: 20 minutes

Serves: 4

Ingredients:
- 6 ounces (170 g) Italian sausage, sliced
- 6 eggs
- ⅛ cup heavy cream
- Salt and ground black pepper, to taste
- 3 ounces (85 g) Parmesan cheese, grated

Directions:
1. Preheat the air fryer to 350°F (177°C). Grease a muffin pan.
2. Put the sliced sausage in the muffin pan.
3. Beat the eggs with the cream in a bowl and season with salt and pepper.
4. Pour half of the mixture over the sausages in the pan.
5. Sprinkle it with cheese and the remaining egg mixture.
6. Bake in the preheated air fryer for 20 minutes or until set.
7. Serve immediately.

Super Easy Bacon Cups

Prep time: 5 minutes
Cook time: 20 minutes
Serves: 2

Ingredients:

- 3 slices bacon, cooked, sliced in half
- 2 slices ham
- 1 slice tomato
- 2 eggs
- 2 teaspoons grated Parmesan cheese
- Salt and ground black pepper, to taste

Directions:

1. Preheat the air fryer to 375°F (191°C).
2. Line 2 greased muffin tins with 3 half-strips of bacon.
3. Put one slice of ham and half slice of tomato in each muffin tin on top of the bacon.
4. Crack one egg on top of the tomato in each muffin tin and sprinkle each with half a teaspoon of grated Parmesan cheese.
5. Sprinkle with salt and ground black pepper, if desired.

6. Bake in the preheated air fryer for 20 minutes.
7. Remove from the air fryer and let cool.
8. Serve warm.

Simple Scotch Eggs

Prep time: 5 minutes
Cook time: 25 minutes
Serves: 4

Ingredients:
- 4 large hard boiled eggs
- 1 (12-ounce / 340-g) package pork sausage
- 8 slices thick-cut bacon

Special Equipment:
- 4 wooden toothpicks, soaked in water for at least 30 minutes

Directions:
1. Slice the sausage into four parts and place each part into a large circle.
2. Put an egg into each circle and wrap it in the sausage.
3. Put in the refrigerator for 1 hour.
4. Preheat the air fryer to 450°F (235°C).
5. Make a cross with two pieces of thick-cut bacon.
6. Put a wrapped egg in the center, fold the bacon over top of the egg, and secure with a toothpick.
7. Air fry in the preheated air fryer for 25 minutes.
8. Serve immediately.

Onion Omelet

Prep time: 10 minutes
Cook time: 12 minutes
Serves: 2

Ingredients:
- 3 eggs
- Salt and ground black pepper, to taste
- ½ teaspoons soy sauce
- 1 large onion, chopped
- 2 tablespoons grated Cheddar cheese
- Cooking spray

Directions:
1. Preheat the air fryer to 355°F (179°C).
2. In a bowl, whisk together the eggs, salt, pepper, and soy sauce.
3. Spritz a small pan with cooking spray.
4. Spread the chopped onion across the bottom of the pan, then transfer the pan to the air fryer.
5. Bake in the preheated air fryer for 6 minutes or until the onion is translucent.
6. Add the egg mixture on top of the onions to coat well.
7. Add the cheese on top, then continue baking for another 6 minutes.
8. Allow to cool before serving.

Parmesan Ranch Risotto

Prep time: 10 minutes
Cook time: 30 minutes
Serves: 2

Ingredients:
- 1 tablespoon olive oil
- 1 clove garlic, minced
- 1 tablespoon unsalted butter
- 1 onion, diced
- ¾ cup Arborio rice
- 2 cups chicken stock, boiling
- ½ cup Parmesan cheese, grated

Directions:
1. Preheat the air fryer to 390°F (199°C).
2. Grease a round baking tin with olive oil and stir in the garlic, butter, and onion.
3. Transfer the tin to the air fryer and bake for 4 minutes.
4. Add the rice and bake for 4 more minutes.
5. Turn the air fryer to 320°F (160°C) and pour in the chicken stock.
6. Cover and bake for 22 minutes.
7. Scatter with cheese and serve.

Classic British Breakfast

Prep time: 5 minutes
Cook time: 25 minutes
Serves: 2

Ingredients:
- 1 cup potatoes, sliced and diced
- 2 cups beans in tomato sauce
- 2 eggs
- 1 tablespoon olive oil
- 1 sausage
- Salt, to taste

Directions:
1. Preheat the air fryer to 390°F (199°C) and allow to warm.
2. Break the eggs onto a baking dish and sprinkle with salt.
3. Lay the beans on the dish, next to the eggs.
4. In a bowl, coat the potatoes with the olive oil.
5. Sprinkle it with salt.
6. Transfer the bowl of potato slices to the air fryer and bake for 10 minutes.
7. Swap out the bowl of potatoes for the dish containing the eggs and beans.
8. Bake for another 10 minutes.

9. Cover the potatoes with parchment paper.
10. Slice up the sausage and throw the slices on top of the beans and eggs.
11. Bake for another 5 minutes.
12. Serve with the potatoes.

Golden Avocado Tempura

Prep time: 5 minutes
Cook time: 10 minutes
Serves: 4

Ingredients:
- ½ cup bread crumbs
- ½ teaspoons salt
- 1 Hass avocado, pitted, peeled and sliced
- Liquid from 1 can white beans

Directions:
1. Preheat the air fryer to 350°F (177°C).
2. Mix the bread crumbs and salt in a shallow bowl until well incorporated.
3. Dip the avocado slices in the bean liquid, then into the bread crumbs.
4. Put the avocados in the air fryer, taking care not to overlap any slices, and air fry for 10 minutes, giving the basket a good shake at the halfway point.
5. Serve immediately.

Kale and Potato Nuggets

Prep time: 10 minutes
Cook time: 18 minutes
Serves: 4

Ingredients:
- 1 teaspoon extra virgin olive oil
- 1 clove garlic, minced
- 4 cups kale, rinsed and chopped
- 2 cups potatoes, boiled and mashed
- ⅛ cup milk
- Salt and ground black pepper, to taste
- Cooking spray

Directions:
1. Preheat the air fryer to 390°F (199°C).
2. In a skillet over medium heat, sauté the garlic in the olive oil, until it turns golden brown.
3. Sauté with the kale for an additional 3 minutes and remove from the heat.
4. Mix the mashed potatoes, kale and garlic in a bowl.
5. Pour in the milk and sprinkle with salt and pepper.
6. Shape the mixture into nuggets and spritz with cooking spray.

7. Put in the air fryer basket and air fry for 15 minutes, flip the nuggets halfway through cooking to make sure the nuggets fry evenly.
8. Serve immediately.

Bacon Hot Dogs

Prep time: 5 minutes

Cook time: 15 minutes

Serves: 4

Ingredients:
- 3 brazilian sausages, cut into 3 equal pieces
- 9 slices bacon
- 1 tablespoon Italian herbs
- Salt and ground black pepper, to taste

Directions:
1. Preheat the air fryer to 355°F (179°C).
2. Take each slice of bacon and wrap around each piece of sausage.
3. Sprinkle it with Italian herbs, salt and pepper.
4. Air fry the sausages in the preheated air fryer for 15 minutes. 4. Serve warm.

Potatoes Lyonnaise

Prep time: 10 minutes
Cook time: 31 minutes
Serves: 4

Ingredients:
- 1 Vidalia onion, sliced
- 1 teaspoon butter, melted
- 1 teaspoon brown sugar
- 2 large russet potatoes (about 1 pound / 454 g in total), sliced ½-inch thick
- 1 tablespoon vegetable oil
- Salt and freshly ground black pepper, to taste

Directions:
1. Preheat the air fryer to 370°F (188°C).
2. Toss the sliced onions, melted butter and brown sugar together in the air fryer basket.
3. Air fry for 8 minutes, shaking the basket occasionally to help the onions cook evenly.
4. While the onions are cooking, bring a saucepan of salted water to a boil on the stovetop.
5. Par-cook the potatoes in boiling water for 3 minutes.
6. Drain the potatoes and pat them dry with a clean kitchen towel.

7. Add the potatoes to the onions in the air fryer basket and drizzle with vegetable oil.
8. Toss to coat the potatoes with the oil and season with salt and freshly ground black pepper.
9. Increase the air fryer temperature to 400°F (204°C) and air fry for 20 minutes, tossing the vegetables a few times during the cooking time to help the potatoes brown evenly.
10. Season with salt and freshly ground black pepper and serve warm.

Hearty Cheddar Biscuits

Prep time: 10 minutes
Cook time: 22 minutes
Serves: Makes 8 biscuits

Ingredients:

- 2⅓ cups self-rising flour
- 2 tablespoons sugar
- ½ cup butter (1 stick), frozen for 15 minutes
- ½ cup grated Cheddar cheese, plus more to melt on top
- 1⅓ cups buttermilk
- 1 cup all-purpose flour, for shaping
- 1 tablespoon butter, melted

Directions:

1. Line a buttered 7-inch metal cake pan with parchment paper or a silicone liner. Combine the flour and sugar in a large mixing bowl.
2. Grate the butter into the flour.
3. Add the grated cheese and stir to coat the cheese and butter with flour.
4. Then add the buttermilk and stir just until you can no longer see streaks of flour.
5. The dough should be quite wet.

6. Spread the all-purpose (not self-rising) flour out on a small cookie sheet.

7. With a spoon, scoop 8 evenly sized balls of dough into the flour, making sure they don't touch each other.

8. With floured hands, coat each dough ball with flour and toss them gently from hand to hand to shake off any excess flour.

9. Put each floured dough ball into the prepared pan, right up next to the other.

10. This will help the biscuits rise, rather than spreading out.

11. Preheat the air fryer to 380°F (193°C).

12. Transfer the cake pan to the basket of the air fryer.

13. Let the ends of the aluminum foil sling hang across the cake pan before returning the basket to the air fryer.

14. Air fry for 20 minutes.

15. Check the biscuits twice to make sure they are not getting too brown on top.

16. If they are, rearrange the aluminum foil strips to cover any brown parts.

17. After 20 minutes, check the biscuits by inserting a toothpick into the center of the biscuits.

18. It should come out clean.

19. If it needs a little more time, continue to air fry for two extra minutes.

20. Brush the tops of the biscuits with some melted butter and sprinkle a little more grated cheese on top if desired.

21. Pop the basket back into the air fryer for another 2 minutes.

22. Remove the cake pan from the air fryer.

23. Let the biscuits cool for just a minute or two and then turn them out onto a plate and pull apart.

24. Serve immediately.

All-in-One Toast

Prep time: 10 minutes

Cook time: 10 minutes

Serves: 1

Ingredients:
- 1 strip bacon, diced
- 1 slice 1-inch thick bread
- 1 egg
- Salt and freshly ground black pepper, to taste
- ¼ cup grated Colby cheese

Directions:
1. Preheat the air fryer to 400°F (204°C).
2. Air fry the bacon for 3 minutes, shaking the basket once or twice while it cooks.
3. Remove the bacon to a paper towel lined plate and set aside.
4. Use a sharp paring knife to score a large circle in the middle of the slice of bread, cutting halfway through, but not all the way through to the cutting board.
5. Press down on the circle in the center of the bread slice to create an indentation.
6. Transfer the slice of bread, hole side up, to the air fryer basket.

7. Crack the egg into the center of the bread, and season with salt and pepper.
8. Adjust the air fryer temperature to 380°F (193°C) and air fry for 5 minutes.
9. Sprinkle the grated cheese around the edges of the bread, leaving the center of the yolk uncovered, and top with the cooked bacon.
10. Press the cheese and bacon into the bread lightly to help anchor it to the bread and prevent it from blowing around in the air fryer.
11. Air fry for one or two more minutes, just to melt the cheese and finish cooking the egg.
12. Serve immediately.

Quick and Easy Blueberry Muffins

Prep time: 10 minutes
Cook time: 12 minutes
Serves: Makes 8 muffins

Ingredients:
- 1⅓ cups flour
- ½ cup sugar
- 2 teaspoons baking powder
- ¼ teaspoon salt
- ⅓ cup canola oil
- 1 egg
- ½ cup milk
- ⅔ cup blueberries, fresh or frozen and thawed

Directions:
1. Preheat the air fryer to 330°F (166°C).
2. In a medium bowl, stir together flour, sugar, baking powder, and salt.
3. In a separate bowl, combine oil, egg, and milk and mix well.
4. Add egg mixture to dry ingredients and stir just until moistened.
5. Gently stir in the blueberries.
6. Spoon batter evenly into parchment-paper-lined muffin cups.

7. Put 4 muffin cups in the air fryer basket and bake for 12 minutes or until the tops spring back when touched lightly.

8. Repeat the previous step to bake the remaining muffins.

9. Serve immediately.

Oat and Chia Porridge

Prep time: 10 minutes
Cook time: 5 minutes
Serves: 4

Ingredients:
- 2 tablespoons peanut butter
- 4 tablespoons honey
- 1 tablespoon butter, melted
- 4 cups milk
- 2 cups oats
- 1 cup chia seeds

Directions:
1. Preheat the air fryer to 390°F (199°C).
2. Put the peanut butter, honey, butter, and milk in a bowl and stir to mix.
3. Add the oats and chia seeds and stir.
4. Transfer the mixture to a bowl and bake in the air fryer for 5 minutes.
5. Give another stir before serving.

Pita and Pepperoni Pizza

Prep time: 10 minutes
Cook time: 6 minutes
Serves: 1

Ingredients:
- 1 teaspoon olive oil
- 1 tablespoon pizza sauce
- 1 pita bread
- 6 pepperoni slices
- ¼ cup grated Mozzarella cheese
- ¼ teaspoon garlic powder
- ¼ teaspoon dried oregano

Directions:
1. Preheat the air fryer to 350°F (177°C). Grease the air fryer basket with olive oil.
2. Spread the pizza sauce on top of the pita bread.
3. Put the pepperoni slices over the sauce, followed by the Mozzarella cheese.
4. Season with garlic powder and oregano.
5. Put the pita pizza inside the air fryer and place a trivet on top.
6. Bake in the preheated air fryer for 6 minutes and serve.

Tomato and Mozzarella Bruschetta

Prep time: 5 minutes
Cook time: 4 minutes
Serves: 1

Ingredients:
- 6 small loaf slices
- ½ cup tomatoes, finely chopped
- 3 ounces (85 g) Mozzarella cheese, grated
- 1 tablespoon fresh basil, chopped
- 1 tablespoon olive oil

Directions:
1. Preheat the air fryer to 350°F (177°C).
2. Put the loaf slices inside the air fryer and air fry for about 3 minutes.
3. Add the tomato, Mozzarella, basil, and olive oil on top.
4. Air fry for an additional minute before serving.

Easy Sausage Pizza

Prep time: 10 minutes

Cook time: 6 minutes

Serves: 4

- 2 tablespoons ketchup
- 1 pita bread
- ⅓ cup sausage
- ½ pound (227 g) Mozzarella cheese
- 1 teaspoon garlic powder
- 1 tablespoon olive oil

Directions:

1. Preheat the air fryer to 340°F (171°C).
2. Spread the ketchup over the pita bread.
3. Top with the sausage and cheese.
4. Sprinkle it with garlic powder and olive oil.
5. Put the pizza in the air fryer basket and bake for 6 minutes.
6. Serve warm.

Simple Cinnamon Toasts

Prep time: 5 minutes
Cook time: 4 minutes
Serves: 4

Ingredients:
- 1 tablespoon salted butter
- 2 teaspoons ground cinnamon
- 4 tablespoons sugar
- ½ teaspoon vanilla extract
- 10 bread slices

Directions:
1. Preheat the air fryer to 380°F (193°C).
2. In a bowl, combine the butter, cinnamon, sugar, and vanilla extract.
3. Spread onto the slices of bread.
4. Put the bread inside the air fryer and bake for 4 minutes or until golden brown.
5. Serve warm.

Gold Avocado

Prep time: 5 minutes
Cook time: 6 minutes
Serves: 4

Ingredients:
- 2 large avocados, sliced
- ¼ teaspoon paprika
- Salt and ground black pepper, to taste
- ½ cup flour
- 2 eggs, beaten
- 1 cup bread crumbs

Directions:
1. Preheat the air fryer to 400°F (204°C).
2. Sprinkle paprika, salt and pepper on the slices of avocado.
3. Lightly coat the avocados with flour.
4. Dredge them in the eggs, before covering with bread crumbs.
5. Transfer to the air fryer and air fry for 6 minutes.
6. Serve warm.

Bacon Eggs on the Go

Prep time: 5 minutes
Cook time: 15 minutes
Serves: 1

Ingredients:
- 2 eggs
- 4 ounces (113 g) bacon, cooked
- Salt and ground black pepper, to taste

Directions:
1. Preheat the air fryer to 400°F (204°C).
2. Put liners in a regular cupcake tin.
3. Crack an egg into each of the cups and add the bacon.
4. Season with some pepper and salt.
5. Bake in the preheated air fryer for 15 minutes, or until the eggs are set.
6. Serve warm.

Pretzels

Prep time: 10 minutes
Cook time: 6 minutes
Serves: Makes 24 pretzels

Ingredients:
- 2 teaspoons yeast
- 1 cup water, warm
- 1 teaspoon sugar
- 1 teaspoon salt
- 2½ cups all-purpose flour
- 2 tablespoons butter, melted, plus more as needed
- 1 cup boiling water
- 1 tablespoon baking soda
- Coarse sea salt, to taste

Directions:
1. Combine the yeast and water in a small bowl.
2. Combine the sugar, salt and flour in the bowl of a stand mixer.
3. With the mixer running and using the dough hook, drizzle in the yeast mixture and melted butter and knead dough until smooth and elastic, about 10 minutes.
4. Shape into a ball and let the dough rise for 1 hour.

5. Punch the dough down to release any air and divide the dough into 24 portions.
6. Roll each portion into a skinny rope using both hands on the counter and rolling from the center to the ends of the rope.
7. Spin the rope into a pretzel shape (or tie the rope into a knot) and place the tied pretzels on a parchment lined baking sheet.
8. Preheat the air fryer to 350°F (177°C).
9. Combine the boiling water and baking soda in a shallow bowl and whisk to dissolve.
10. Let the water cool so you can put your hands in it.
11. Working in batches, dip the pretzels (top side down) into the baking soda mixture and let them soak for 30 seconds to a minute.
12. Then remove the pretzels carefully and return them (top side up) to the baking sheet.
13. Sprinkle the coarse salt on the top.
14. Air fry in batches for 3 minutes per side.
15. When the pretzels are finished, brush them generously with the melted butter and enjoy them warm.

Sourdough Croutons

Prep time: 5 minutes
Cook time: 6 minutes
Serves: Makes 4 cups

Ingredients:
- 4 cups cubed sourdough bread, 1-inch cubes
- 1 tablespoon olive oil
- 1 teaspoon fresh thyme leaves
- ¼ teaspoon salt
- Freshly ground black pepper, to taste

Directions:
1. Combine all ingredients in a bowl.
2. Preheat the air fryer to 400°F (204°C).
3. Toss the bread cubes into the air fryer and air fry for 6 minutes, shaking the basket once or twice while they cook.
4. Serve warm.

Spinach Omelet

Prep time: 10 minutes
Cook time: 10 minutes
Serves: 1

Ingredients:
- 1 teaspoon olive oil
- 3 eggs
- Salt and ground black pepper, to taste
- 1 tablespoon ricotta cheese
- ¼ cup chopped spinach
- 1 tablespoon chopped parsley

Directions:
1. Grease the air fryer basket with olive oil.
2. Preheat the air fryer to 330°F (166°C).
3. In a bowl, beat the eggs with a fork and sprinkle salt and pepper.
4. Add the ricotta, spinach, and parsley and then transfer to the air fryer.
5. Bake for 10 minutes or until the egg is set.
6. Serve warm.

Fast Coffee Donuts

Prep time: 5 minutes
Cook time: 6 minutes
Serves: 6

Ingredients:

- ¼ cup sugar
- ½ teaspoon salt
- 1 cup flour
- 1 teaspoon baking powder
- ¼ cup coffee
- 1 tablespoon aquafaba
- 1 tablespoon sunflower oil

Directions:

1. In a large bowl, combine the sugar, salt, flour, and baking powder.
2. Add the coffee, aquafaba, and sunflower oil and mix until a dough is formed.
3. Leave the dough to rest in the refrigerator.
4. Preheat the air fryer to 400°F (204°C).
5. Remove the dough from the fridge and divide up, kneading each section into a doughnut.

6. Put the doughnuts inside the air fryer. Air fry for 6 minutes.
7. Serve immediately.

Cornflakes Toast Sticks

Prep time: 10 minutes
Cook time: 6 minutes
Serves: 4

Ingredients:
- 2 eggs
- ½ cup milk
- ⅛ teaspoon salt
- ½ teaspoon pure vanilla extract
- ¾ cup crushed cornflakes
- 6 slices sandwich bread, each slice cut into 4 strips
- Maple syrup, for dipping
- Cooking spray

Directions:
1. Preheat the air fryer to 390°F (199°C).
2. In a small bowl, beat together the eggs, milk, salt, and vanilla.
3. Put crushed cornflakes on a plate or in a shallow dish.
4. Dip bread strips in egg mixture, shake off excess, and roll in cornflake crumbs.
5. Spray both sides of bread strips with oil.
6. Put bread strips in an air fryer basket in a single layer.

7. Air fry for 6 minutes or until golden brown.
8. Repeat steps 5 and 6 to air fry remaining French toast sticks.
9. Serve with maple syrup.

PB&J

Prep time: 5 minutes
Cook time: 6 minutes
Serves: 4

Ingredients:
- ½ cup cornflakes, crushed
- ¼ cup shredded coconut
- 8 slices oat nut bread or any whole-grain, oversize bread
- 6 tablespoons peanut butter
- 2 medium bananas, cut into ½-inch-thick slices
- 6 tablespoons pineapple preserves
- 1 egg, beaten
- Cooking spray

Directions:
1. Preheat the air fryer to 360°F (182°C).
2. In a shallow dish, mix the cornflake crumbs and coconut.
3. For each sandwich, spread one bread slice with 1½ tablespoons of peanut butter.
4. Top with banana slices.
5. Spread another bread slice with 1½ tablespoons of preserves.
6. Combine to make a sandwich.

7. Using a pastry brush, brush the top of the sandwich lightly with beaten egg.
8. Sprinkle about 1½ tablespoons of crumb coating, pressing it in to make it stick.
9. Spray with cooking spray.
10. Turn the sandwich over and repeat to coat and spray the other side.
11. Air fry 2 at a time, place sandwiches in an air fryer basket and air fry for 6 minutes or until the coating is golden brown and crispy.
12. Cut the cooked sandwiches in half and serve warm.

Buttermilk Biscuits

Prep time: 5 minutes
Cook time: 5 minutes
Serves: Makes 12 biscuits

Ingredients:
- 2 cups all-purpose flour, plus more for dusting the work surface
- 1 tablespoon baking powder
- ¼ teaspoon baking soda
- 2 teaspoons sugar
- 1 teaspoon salt
- 6 tablespoons cold unsalted butter, cut into 1-tablespoon slices
- ¾ cup buttermilk

Directions:
1. Preheat the air fryer to 360°F (182°C). Spray the air fryer basket with olive oil.
2. In a large mixing bowl, combine the flour, baking powder, baking soda, sugar, and salt and mix well.
3. Using a fork, cut in the butter until the mixture resembles coarse meal.
4. Add the buttermilk and mix until smooth.
5. Dust more flour on a clean work surface.

6. Turn the dough out onto the work surface and roll it out until it is about ½ inch thick.
7. Using a 2-inch biscuit cutter, cut out the biscuits.
8. Put the uncooked biscuits in the greased air fryer basket in a single layer.
9. Bake for 5 minutes.
10. Transfer the cooked biscuits from the air fryer to a platter.
11. Cut the remaining biscuits.
12. Bake the remaining biscuits.
13. Serve warm.

Banana Churros with Oatmeal

Prep time: 15 minutes
Cook time: 15 minutes
Serves: 2

Ingredients:

For the Churros:

- 1 large yellow banana, peeled, cut in half lengthwise, then cut in half widthwise
- 2 tablespoons whole-wheat pastry flour
- ⅛ teaspoon sea salt
- 2 teaspoons oil (sunflower or melted coconut)
- 1 teaspoon water
- Cooking spray
- 1 tablespoon coconut sugar
- ½ teaspoon cinnamon

For the Oatmeal:

- ¾ cup rolled oats
- 1½ cups water

Directions:

To make the churros:

1. Put the 4 banana pieces in a medium-size bowl and add the flour and salt.
2. Stir gently.

3. Add the oil and water.
4. Stir gently until evenly mixed.
5. You may need to press some coating onto the banana pieces.
6. Spray the air fryer basket with the oil spray.
7. Put the banana pieces in the air fryer basket and air fry for 5 minutes.
8. Remove, gently turn over, and air fry for another 5 minutes or until browned.
9. In a medium bowl, add the coconut sugar and cinnamon and stir to combine.
10. When the banana pieces are nicely browned, spray with the oil and place in the cinnamon-sugar bowl.
11. Toss gently with a spatula to coat the banana pieces with the mixture.

To make the oatmeal:
1. While the bananas are cooking, make the oatmeal.
2. In a medium pot, bring the oats and water to a boil, then reduce to low heat.
3. Simmer, stirring often, until all the water is absorbed, about 5 minutes.
4. Put the oatmeal into two bowls.
5. Top the oatmeal with the coated banana pieces and serve immediately.

Lush Vegetable Omelet

Prep time: 10 minutes

Cook time: 13 minutes

Serves: 2

Ingredients:
- 2 teaspoons canola oil
- 4 eggs, whisked
- 3 tablespoons plain milk
- 1 teaspoon melted butter
- 1 red bell pepper, seeded and chopped
- 1 green bell pepper, seeded and chopped
- 1 white onion, finely chopped
- ½ cup baby spinach leaves, roughly chopped
- ½ cup Halloumi cheese, shaved
- Kosher salt and freshly ground black pepper, to taste

Directions:
1. Preheat the air fryer to 350°F (177°C).
2. Grease a baking pan with canola oil.
3. Put the remaining ingredients in the baking pan and stir well.
4. Transfer to the air fryer and bake for 13 minutes.
5. Serve warm.

Spinach with Scrambled Eggs

Prep time: 10 minutes
Cook time: 10 minutes
Serves: 2

Ingredients:
- 2 tablespoons olive oil
- 4 eggs, whisked
- 5 ounces (142 g) fresh spinach, chopped
- 1 medium tomato, chopped
- 1 teaspoon fresh lemon juice
- ½ teaspoon coarse salt
- ½ teaspoon ground black pepper
- ½ cup of fresh basil, roughly chopped

Directions:
1. Grease a baking pan with the oil, tilting it to spread the oil around.
2. Preheat the air fryer to 280ºF (138ºC).
3. Mix the remaining ingredients, apart from the basil leaves, whisking well until everything is completely combined.
4. Bake in the air fryer for 10 minutes.
5. Top with fresh basil leaves before serving.

English Pumpkin Egg Bake

Prep time: 10 minutes
Cook time: 10 minutes
Serves: 2

Ingredients:

- 2 eggs
- ½ cup milk
- 2 cups flour
- 2 tablespoons cider vinegar
- 2 teaspoons baking powder
- 1 tablespoon sugar
- 1 cup pumpkin purée
- 1 teaspoon cinnamon powder
- 1 teaspoon baking soda
- 1 tablespoon olive oil

Directions:

1. Preheat the air fryer to 300°F (149°C).
2. Crack the eggs into a bowl and beat with a whisk.
3. Combine with the milk, flour, cider vinegar, baking powder, sugar, pumpkin purée, cinnamon powder, and baking soda, mixing well.
4. Grease a baking tray with oil.

5. Add the mixture and transfer into the air fryer.
6. Bake for 10 minutes.
7. Serve warm.

Mushroom and Squash Toast

Prep time: 10 minutes
Cook time: 10 minutes
Serves: 4

Ingredients:

- 1 tablespoon olive oil
- 1 red bell pepper, cut into strips
- 2 green onions, sliced
- 1 cup sliced button or cremini mushrooms
- 1 small yellow squash, sliced
- 2 tablespoons softened butter
- 4 slices bread
- ½ cup soft goat cheese

Directions:

1. Brush the air fryer basket with the olive oil and preheat the air fryer to 350°F (177°C).
2. Put the red pepper, green onions, mushrooms, and squash inside the air fryer, give them a stir and air fry for 7 minutes or the vegetables are tender, shaking the basket once throughout the cooking time.
3. Remove the vegetables and set them aside.

4. Spread the butter on the slices of bread and transfer to the air fryer, butter-side up. Brown for 3 minutes.
5. Remove the toast from the air fryer and top with goat cheese and vegetables. Serve warm.

Potato Bread Rolls

Prep time: 15 minutes

Cook time: 20 minutes

Serves: 5

Ingredients:
- 5 large potatoes, boiled and mashed
- Salt and ground black pepper, to taste
- ½ teaspoon mustard seeds
- 1 tablespoon olive oil
- 2 small onions, chopped
- 2 sprigs curry leaves
- ½ teaspoon turmeric powder
- 2 green chilis, seeded and chopped
- 1 bunch coriander, chopped
- 8 slices bread, brown sides discarded

Directions:
1. Preheat the air fryer to 400°F (204°C).
2. Put the mashed potatoes in a bowl and sprinkle on salt and pepper.
3. Set to one side.
4. Fry the mustard seeds in olive oil over a medium-low heat in a skillet, stirring continuously, until they sputter.
5. Add the onions and cook until they turn translucent.

6. Add the curry leaves and turmeric powder and stir.

7. Cook for a further 2 minutes until fragrant.

8. Remove the pan from the heat and combine with the potatoes.

9. Mix in the green chilies and coriander.

10. Wet the bread slightly and drain off any excess liquid.

11. Spoon a small amount of the potato mixture into the center of the bread and enclose the bread around the filling, sealing it entirely.

12. Continue until the rest of the bread and filling is used up.

13. Brush each bread roll with some oil and transfer to the basket of the air fryer.

14. Air fry for 15 minutes, gently shaking the air fryer basket at the halfway point to ensure each roll is cooked evenly.

15. Serve immediately.

Soufflé

Prep time: 10 minutes
Cook time: 22 minutes
Serves: 4

Ingredients:
- ⅓ cup butter, melted
- ¼ cup flour
- 1 cup milk
- 1 ounce (28 g) sugar
- 4 egg yolks
- 1 teaspoon vanilla extract
- 6 egg whites
- 1 teaspoon cream of tartar
- Cooking spray

Directions:
1. In a bowl, mix the butter and flour until a smooth consistency is achieved.
2. Pour the milk into a saucepan over medium-low heat.
3. Add the sugar and allow to dissolve before raising the heat to boil the milk.
4. Pour in the flour and butter mixture and stir vigorously for 7 minutes to eliminate any lumps.
5. Make sure the mixture thickens.

6. Take off the heat and let it cool for 15 minutes.
7. Preheat the air fryer to 320°F (160°C).
8. Spritz 6 soufflé dishes with cooking spray.
9. Put the egg yolks and vanilla extract in a separate bowl and beat them together with a fork.
10. Pour in the milk and combine well to incorporate everything.
11. In a smaller bowl mix the egg whites and cream of tartar with a fork.
12. Fold into the egg yolks-milk mixture before adding in the flour mixture.
13. Transfer equal amounts to the 6 soufflé dishes.
14. Put the dishes in the air fryer and bake for 15 minutes.
15. Serve warm.

Creamy Cinnamon Rolls

Prep time: 10 minutes
Cook time: 9 minutes
Serves: 8

Ingredients:
- 1 pound (454 g) frozen bread dough, thawed
- ¼ cup butter, melted
- ¾ cup brown sugar
- 1½ tablespoons ground cinnamon

Cream Cheese Glaze:
- 4 ounces (113 g) cream cheese, softened
- 2 tablespoons butter, softened
- 1¼ cups powdered sugar
- ½ teaspoon vanilla extract

Directions:
1. Let the bread dough come to room temperature on the counter.
2. On a lightly floured surface, roll the dough into a 13-inch by 11-inch rectangle.
3. Position the rectangle so the 13-inch side is facing you.

4. Brush the melted butter all over the dough, leaving a 1-inch border uncovered along the edge farthest away from you.
5. Combine the brown sugar and cinnamon in a small bowl.
6. Sprinkle the mixture evenly over the buttered dough, keeping the 1-inch border uncovered.
7. Roll the dough into a log, starting with the edge closest to you.
8. Roll the dough tightly, rolling evenly, and push out any air pockets.
9. When you get to the uncovered edge of the dough, press the dough onto the roll to seal it together.
10. Cut the log into 8 pieces, slicing slowly with a sawing motion so you don't flatten the dough.
11. Turn the slices on their sides and cover with a clean kitchen towel.
12. Let the rolls sit in the warmest part of the kitchen for 1½ to 2 hours to rise.
13. To make the glaze, place the cream cheese and butter in a microwave safe bowl.
14. Soften the mixture in the microwave for 30 seconds at a time until it is easy to stir.
15. Gradually add the powdered sugar and stir to combine.
16. Add the vanilla extract and whisk until smooth. Set aside.

17. When the rolls have risen, preheat the air fryer to 350°F (177°C).
18. Transfer 4 of the rolls to the air fryer basket.
19. Air fry for 5 minutes.
20. Turn the rolls over and air fry for another 4 minutes.
21. Repeat with the remaining 4 rolls.
22. Let the rolls cool for two minutes before glazing.
23. Spread large dollops of cream cheese glaze on top of the warm cinnamon rolls, allowing some glaze to drip down the side of the rolls.
24. Serve warm.

Bacon and Broccoli Bread Pudding

Prep time: 15 minutes
Cook time: 48 minutes
Serves: 2 to 4

Ingredients:
- ½ pound (227 g) thick cut bacon, cut into ¼-inch pieces
- 3 cups brioche bread, cut into ½-inch cubes
- 2 tablespoons butter, melted
- 3 eggs
- 1 cup milk
- ½ teaspoon salt
- Freshly ground black pepper, to taste
- 1 cup frozen broccoli florets, thawed and chopped
- 1½ cups grated Swiss cheese

Directions:
1. Preheat the air fryer to 400°F (204°C).
2. Air fry the bacon for 8 minutes until crispy, shaking the basket a few times to help it air fry evenly.
3. Remove the bacon and set it aside on a paper towel.
4. Air fry the brioche bread cubes for 2 minutes to dry and toast lightly.
5. Butter a cake pan.

6. Combine all the ingredients in a large bowl and toss well.
7. Transfer the mixture to the buttered cake pan, cover with aluminum foil and refrigerate the bread pudding overnight, or for at least 8 hours.
8. Remove the cake pan from the refrigerator an hour before you plan to bake and let it sit on the countertop to come to room temperature.
9. Preheat the air fryer to 330°F (166°C).
10. Transfer the covered cake pan to the basket of the air fryer, lowering the pan into the basket.
11. Fold the ends of the aluminum foil over the top of the pan before returning the basket to the air fryer.
12. 7. Air fry for 20 minutes.
13. Remove the foil and air fry for an additional 20 minutes.
14. If the top browns a little too much before the custard has set, simply return the foil to the pan.
15. The bread pudding is cooked through when a skewer inserted into the center comes out clean.
16. Serve warm.

Grit and Ham Fritters

Prep time: 15 minutes
Cook time: 20 minutes
Serves: 6 to 8

Ingredients:
- 4 cups water
- 1 cup quick-cooking grits
- ¼ teaspoon salt
- 2 tablespoons butter
- 2 cups grated Cheddar cheese, divided
- 1 cup finely diced ham
- 1 tablespoon chopped chives
- Salt and freshly ground black pepper, to taste
- 1 egg, beaten
- 2 cups panko bread crumbs
- Cooking spray

Directions:
1. Bring the water to a boil in a saucepan.
2. Whisk in the grits and ¼ teaspoon of salt, and cook for 7 minutes until the grits are soft.
3. Remove the pan from the heat and stir in the butter and 1 cup of the grated Cheddar cheese.
4. Transfer the grits to a bowl and let them cool for 10 to 15 minutes.

5. Stir the ham, chives and the rest of the cheese into the grits and season with salt and pepper to taste.
6. Add the beaten egg and refrigerate the mixture for 30 minutes.
7. Put the panko bread crumbs in a shallow dish.
8. Measure out ¼-cup portions of the grits mixture and shape them into patties.
9. Coat all sides of the patties with the panko bread crumbs, patting them with the hands so the crumbs adhere to the patties.
10. You should have about 16 patties.
11. Spritz both sides of the patties with cooking spray.
12. Preheat the air fryer to 400°F (204°C).
13. In batches of 5 or 6, air fry the fritters for 8 minutes.
14. Using a flat spatula, flip the fritters over and air fry for another 4 minutes.
15. Serve hot.

Apple and Walnut Muffins

Prep time: 15 minutes
Cook time: 10 minutes
Serves: Makes 8 muffins

Ingredients:
- 1 cup flour
- ⅓ cup sugar
- 1 teaspoon baking powder
- ¼ teaspoon baking soda
- ¼ teaspoon salt
- 1 teaspoon cinnamon
- ¼ teaspoon ginger
- ¼ teaspoon nutmeg
- 1 egg
- 2 tablespoons pancake syrup, plus 2 teaspoons
- 2 tablespoons melted butter, plus 2 teaspoons
- ¾ cup unsweetened applesauce
- ½ teaspoon vanilla extract
- ¼ cup chopped walnuts
- ¼ cup diced apple

Directions:
1. Preheat the air fryer to 330°F (166°C).

2. In a large bowl, stir together the flour, sugar, baking powder, baking soda, salt, cinnamon, ginger, and nutmeg.
3. In a small bowl, beat the egg until frothy.
4. Add syrup, butter, applesauce, and vanilla and mix well.
5. Pour egg mixture into dry ingredients and stir just until moistened.
6. Gently stir in nuts and diced apple.
7. Divide batter among 8 parchment-paper-lined muffin cups.
8. Put 4 muffin cups in the air fryer basket and bake for 10 minutes.
9. Repeat with remaining 4 muffins or until the toothpick inserted in the center comes out clean.
10. Serve warm.

Ham and Corn Muffins

Prep time: 10 minutes
Cook time: 6 minutes
Serves: Makes 8 muffins

Ingredients:
- ¾ cup yellow cornmeal
- ¼ cup flour
- 1½ teaspoons baking powder
- ¼ teaspoon salt
- 1 egg, beaten
- 2 tablespoons canola oil
- ½ cup milk
- ½ cup shredded sharp Cheddar cheese
- ½ cup diced ham

Directions:
1. Preheat the air fryer to 390°F (199°C).
2. In a medium bowl, stir together the cornmeal, flour, baking powder, and salt.
3. Add the egg, oil, and milk to dry ingredients and mix well.
4. Stir in shredded cheese and diced ham.
5. Divide batter among 8 parchment-paper-lined muffin cups.

6. Put 4 filled muffin cups in the air fryer basket and bake for 5 minutes.
7. Reduce temperature to 330°F (166°C) and bake for 1 minute or until a toothpick inserted in the center of the muffin comes out clean.
8. Repeat steps 6 and 7 to bake remaining muffins.
9. Serve warm.

Nut and Seed Muffins

Prep time: 15 minutes
Cook time: 10 minutes
Serves: Makes 8 muffins

Ingredients:

- ½ cup whole-wheat flour, plus 2 tablespoons
- ¼ cup oat bran F
- 2 tablespoons flaxseed meal
- ¼ cup brown sugar
- ½ teaspoon baking soda
- ½ teaspoon baking powder
- ¼ teaspoon salt
- ½ teaspoon cinnamon
- ½ cup buttermilk
- 2 tablespoons melted butter
- 1 egg
- ½ teaspoon pure vanilla extract
- ½ cup grated carrots
- ¼ cup chopped pecans
- ¼ cup chopped walnuts
- 1 tablespoon pumpkin seeds
- 1 tablespoon sunflower seeds
- Cooking spray

Special Equipment:

- 16 foil muffin cups, paper liners removed

Directions:
1. Preheat the air fryer to 330°F (166°C).
2. In a large bowl, stir together the flour, bran, flaxseed meal, sugar, baking soda, baking powder, salt, and cinnamon.
3. In a medium bowl, beat together the buttermilk, butter, egg, and vanilla.
4. Pour into the flour mixture and stir just until the dry ingredients moisten.
5. Do not beat.
6. Gently stir in carrots, nuts, and seeds.
7. Double up the foil cups so you have 8 total and spritz with cooking spray.
8. Put 4 foil cups in the air fryer basket and divide half the batter among them.
9. Bake for 10 minutes or until a toothpick inserted in the center comes out clean.
10. Repeat step 7 to bake the remaining 4 muffins.
11. Serve warm.

Posh Orange Rolls

Prep time: 15 minutes
Cook time: 8 minutes
Serves: Makes 8 rolls

Ingredients:
- 3 ounces (85 g) low-fat cream cheese
- 1 tablespoon low-fat sour cream or plain yogurt
- 2 teaspoons sugar
- ¼ teaspoon pure vanilla extract
- ¼ teaspoon orange extract
- 1 can (8 count) organic crescent roll dough
- ¼ cup chopped walnuts
- ¼ cup dried cranberries
- ¼ cup shredded, sweetened coconut
- Butter-flavored cooking spray

Orange Glaze:
- ½ cup powdered sugar
- 1 tablespoon orange juice
- ¼ teaspoon orange extract
- Dash of salt

Directions:
1. Cut a circular piece of parchment paper slightly smaller than the bottom of the air fryer basket. Set aside.

2. In a small bowl, combine the cream cheese, sour cream or yogurt, sugar, and vanilla and orange extracts. Stir until smooth.

3. Preheat the air fryer to 300°F (149°C).

4. Separate crescent roll dough into 8 triangles and divide cream cheese mixture among them.

5. Starting at the wide end, spread the cheese mixture to within 1 inch of point.

6. Sprinkle nuts and cranberries evenly over the cheese mixture.

7. Starting at the wide end, roll up triangles, then sprinkle with coconut, pressing in lightly to make it stick.

8. Spray tops of rolls with butter flavored cooking spray.

9. Put parchment paper in the air fryer basket, and place 4 rolls on top, spaced evenly.

10. Air fry for 8 minutes, until rolls are golden brown and cooked through.

11. Repeat steps 7 and 8 to air fry the remaining 4 rolls.

12. You should be able to use the same piece of parchment paper twice.

13. In a small bowl, stir together ingredients for glaze and drizzle over warm rolls.

14. Serve warm.

Avocado Quesadillas

Prep time: 10 minutes
Cook time: 11 minutes
Serves: 4

Ingredients:
- 4 eggs
- 2 tablespoons skim milk
- Salt and ground black pepper, to taste
- Cooking spray
- 4 flour tortillas
- 4 tablespoons salsa
- 2 ounces (57 g) Cheddar cheese, grated
- ½ small avocado, peeled and thinly sliced

Ingredients:
1. Preheat the air fryer to 270°F (132°C).
2. Beat together the eggs, milk, salt, and pepper.
3. Spray a baking pan lightly with cooking spray and add egg mixture.
4. Bake for 8 minutes, stirring every 1 to 2 minutes, until eggs are scrambled to the liking.
5. Remove and set aside.
6. Spray one side of each tortilla with cooking spray.
7. Flip over.

8. Divide eggs, salsa, cheese, and avocado among the tortillas, covering only half of each tortilla.
9. Fold each tortilla in half and press down lightly.
10. Increase the temperature of the air fryer to 390°F (199°C).
11. Put 2 tortillas in an air fryer basket and air fry for 3 minutes or until the cheese melts and the outside feels slightly crispy.
12. Repeat with the remaining two tortillas.
13. Cut each cooked tortilla into halves.
14. Serve warm.

Banana Bread

Prep time: 10 minutes

Cook time: 22 minutes

Serves: Makes 3 loaves

Ingredients:
- 3 ripe bananas, mashed
- 1 cup sugar
- 1 large egg
- 4 tablespoons (½ stick) unsalted butter, melted
- 1½ cups all-purpose flour
- 1 teaspoon baking soda
- 1 teaspoon salt

Directions:
1. Coat the insides of 3 mini loaf pans with cooking spray.
2. In a large mixing bowl, mix the bananas and sugar.
3. In a separate large mixing bowl, combine the egg, butter, flour, baking soda, and salt and mix well.
4. Add the banana mixture to the egg and flour mixture.
5. Mix well.
6. Divide the batter evenly among the prepared pans.
7. Preheat the air fryer to 310°F (154°C). Set the mini loaf pans into the air fryer basket.
8. Bake in the preheated air fryer for 22 minutes.

9. Insert a toothpick into the center of each loaf; if it comes out clean, they are done.
10. When the loaves are cooked through, remove the pans from the air fryer basket.
11. Turn out the loaves onto a wire rack to cool.
12. Serve warm.

Notes

CPSIA information can be obtained
at www.ICGtesting.com
Printed in the USA
LVHW080817300721
693916LV00002B/103

9 781803 398082